IMPROVING YOUR GAME

How to Succeed in
Medical Device Sales

Ray Oktavec & John Spranger

About The Authors

Ray Oktavec

Ray is currently Director of the Surgical Innovation Team at DePuy Synthes Spine, a Johnson & Johnson company. As top performer in a variety of sales positions, Ray leads by example. He sets high expectations for his team and always has a plan with goals that he can measure throughout the sales process.

His responsibilities include training sales representatives and surgeons, as well as providing solutions for complex and minimally invasive spinal procedures. Ray also recently received a U.S. patent for one of his inventions to facilitate minimally invasive spine surgery.

In the past Ray has also worked for other companies, such as Abbott Laboratories and Nuvasive Spine. Whether he's with a young start-up or a Fortune 100 company, Ray knows the principles of the sale remain the same.

Ray is one of four children, raised in Fort Lauderdale, Florida. Ray learned the art of sales at his father's side from an early age. Over summer vacations, he enjoyed traveling with his salesman father to make sales calls at national meetings and conferences.

Ray has been a leader all his life. He was a captain on the football field at Mississippi College, where he lettered for four years. Ray is also active in his community. From 2004 to 2015, he served with the Associated Marine Institute (AMI Kids), Greater Ft. Lauderdale, a non-profit in Broward County. He was Chairman of the Board for two years.

Ray loves to attend professional sporting events around the country. He is a fan of all things outdoors, including big-game hunting, fishing, and snowboarding. Ray's energy can best be described with a single word: passion. This quality permeates everything he does and drives him to fulfill his potential to the utmost.

John Spranger

John came to medical device sales from a previous career in clinical work. He was an accomplished Physician Assistant, working in neurosurgery, as well as deformity and complex orthopedic spine surgery.

An expert in consultative selling, John quickly distinguished himself as a leader in medical device sales. He is currently Specialty Sales Director for Depuy Synthes Spine, a Johnson & Johnson company. He works closely with his team of managers to sell, influence and teach the sales force. His mission is to improve their sales acumen clinically, technically, and deftly.

John was raised in a small Wisconsin town. He currently resides in Denver with his wife and two young daughters. An avid outdoor sports enthusiast, John loves mountain biking, skiing, cycling, and hiking. He is a three-time ironman finisher, as well as an instrument-rated pilot.

An Ideal Partnership

Since Ray Oktavec and John Spranger arrived at similar places in their careers via very different routes, their respective styles complement each other well. Through their professional association, they have helped each other develop into expert medical device sales professionals.

In the course of their combined 33-plus years of experience in the healthcare, pharmaceutical and medical device fields, Ray and John have interviewed hundreds of professionals for medical device sales opportunities. Their responsibilities have spanned the local, regional and national arenas.

Ray and John have seen their share of sales challenges and sales successes. They know full well what it takes to be a stellar medical device sales representative.

Better yet, they are happy to share their combined knowledge, in order to help you achieve your highest, true excellence in medical device sales.

Acknowledgments

This book could not be possible without the help and support of so many people in my life. I am very thankful to all of you. The list is way too long to share here, but here is the short version:

First, I would like to thank John for his dedication and commitment in writing this book. Together, we did something both of us had only talked about.

Second, I would like to thank Depuy Synthes Spine and Johnson & Johnson for allowing us to write about our professional journey in the healthcare industry. It's been a privilege to share many of the values, principles and techniques we have learned along the way.

Last, and most important, I would like to thank my family and friends for everything they have done for me in my life. I learned so much about all that's good from my parents, two sisters, brother, and dear friends.

Mom and Dad, I am so thankful for all the sacrifices and commitment you made for me and for the rest of our family. You always put us first. The love and values you instilled in us are the greatest gift anyone could ever ask for. Thank you for always being there. I love you both very much.

Ray Oktavec

To Erin, Eloise, and Emme, thank you from the bottom of my heart for all your patience through the many sacrifices my career has presented to our family.

Girls, I couldn't have done it without your love and support. I appreciate your belief in me, as well as your unwavering love along the way.

John Spranger

Contents

Preface

How can you become a better medical device sales representative? What are you doing today to improve your skills for tomorrow? What are your goals for next week, next month, next year?

Do you have a plan? Can you articulate it, execute it, and measure your success objectively? What steps are you taking to execute it? Besides a plan, do you have a strategy?

If you are one of the elite few who has developed a professional improvement strategy, what kind of strategy is it?

Is it a comfortable strategy that keeps you moving forward at a steady, but average pace? Or is it an uncomfortable strategy, that will get you to the top of your game now?

Tip!

Perhaps you've already noticed we ask you a lot of questions. Please, for your own sake, pause with each question and reflect. Then give an honest answer. This is how you will truly learn and improve the quickest.

There are no magic secrets in this book. It's full of practical, down-to-earth information, organized in a seamless way to help you unlock your potential as a Sales Representative.

This book can't do the work for you, but it can make your work easier, as you develop a proactive strategy. You can learn to work smart, not hard. This book, if you use it, can teach you to win and maintain a very big book of business.

In these pages, we share how, in our combined and varied careers, we have both won and lost at the sales game…and learned along the way.

We can help shorten your timeline to success. If you take this knowledge and run with it, you will create a more reproducible and predictable sales cycle for yourself. Your success rate will improve and the length of your sales cycle will decrease.

Want to increase your earning potential and your odds of success? Use this book!

We use sports analogies throughout this book. Andy Molinsky, writing for *Harvard Business Review*, February, 2016, in the article "Practice for Tough Situations as You'd Practice a Sport," commented: "One key tenet of professonal sports coaching, for example, is to prepare people in the most realistic contexts possible. When professional football teams prepare for their next opponent, they'll take into account the likely conditions they'll face."

Introduction

Over the course of our combined careers, we have seen many amazing people both succeed and fail in medical device sales. We realized it usually wasn't about individual aptitude, looks, charm or personality.

Success or failure was almost always a result of whether the sales rep could strategize, prepare, and execute according to the right plan. Eventually, we became good at predicting who was going to succeed by paying attention to their focus on planning and follow-through. That's a skill you can learn, practice and improve with the help of this book.

Success can be defined in many ways

We define it as a shorter sales cycle to product use or conversion...culminating in more money in your bank account. This book takes you through all the components to develop your own personal, professional plan and strategy. You will learn how to challenge yourself step-by-step to become, not just a good, but a great, medical device sales rep. It's time to get out of your comfort zone and envision the possibility of greatness.

The medical device sales landscape ia evolving rapidly. The first step is to see how you, the individual sales rep, fit into the ever-changing foggy future.

Here's a hint: The successful sales rep will be an invaluable partner to his or her customer.

He or she will be a consultant, who sees their role as primarily to assist doctors and staff deliver the best outcomes to their patients...not just to sell products.

Consultative sales requires you to be prepared. You must be armed with knowledge that enables you to take full advantage of your opportunities, wherever and whenever they arise.

Time management is an important part of your plan. Learn to spend your time intelligently and strategically. As you shorten your sales cycle, you'll see...time really is money.

Your company wants you to succeed. Their success depends on yours. Your customers want the best products and the best outcomes. Everyone is depending on you to be the middle-man in the process and help everyone else be successful.

Have you used your company's resources to their fullest? Do you even know all that is available? Have you fully tapped into your current customer base to understand their needs?

Your customers' needs are likely the same as many of their colleagues' needs. Understand one and you may understand many more. We will teach you how to identify your best resources and take full advantage of them.

We will explore in depth the art of the sale, all the

way through the execution of your plan.

How do the hundreds of successful medical device sales reps we have seen do it? How do we do it? It's not a secret. We will teach you.

We will also give you the confidence to stay ahead of your competition, no matter how good they are. Planning and preparation are vital here as well.

In everything you do, remember to play by the rules. The medical device industry is subject to tight regulation. Crossing clearly defined lines is costly.

We break down all this information into easily digested chunks. You can gradually phase it into your current work style or jump in all at once, whichever is your preference.

Belief and Preparation

Question: How is that guy with a weak bag of widgets kicking your ass with your customer base?

The answer lies in you.

To sell successfully, you must believe in both your company and your products. If you can't believe in what you sell, how can your customers?

Know everything about your product, and consider every objection you might face. Be confidently prepared for anything.

How prepared are you?

One sales manager we know tells the story of how he arrived at a product training session he was to give for a new iPad app his company had spent a lot of time and money to develop. Twelve seemingly eager sales reps were there to learn how to use it. But out of the twelve, only two had already bothered to download the new app on their iPads.

Would you have been one of the elite two?

The other ten probably never even thought about whether they should prepare. They were just drifting comfortably through their workdays. And now they've ended up in this book as an example of what not to do.

If you are presently one of the slackers, this is your opportunity to start excelling. Take this opportunity and change your life.

Chapter 1

The Successful Medical Device Sales Representative

What does he or she really do?

In the field of medical devices sales, the sales rep who closes the most deals functions more as a consultant than a sales person. He or she brings added value to the patient, hospital and doctor (Patient, Hospital and Doctor, or PHD). This makes all the difference in decision-making. Aligning the values, features and benefits with the PHDs in all your selling scenarios will increase your sales output.

How Do You Rate?

The Michelin Guide has been a top rating system for over a hundred years. Covert inspectors visit restaurants to evaluate their offerings, according to a strict set of criteria: product quality, flavor mastery, cooking mastery, personality of the cuisine, value, and consistency.

The Guide's ratings range from one star to three stars, with the following parameters:

One star: A very good restaurant in its category, offering cuisine prepared to a consistently high standard.

Two stars: Excellent cuisine, skillfully and carefully crafted dishes of outstanding quality. Worth a detour.

Three stars: Exceptional cuisine where diners eat extremely well, often superbly. Distinctive dishes are precisely executed, using superlative ingredients.

A Michelin-rated restaurant uses its star rating to set itself apart and to market its value. The gain or loss of a single star can have a dramatic effect on a restaurant's success.

As a sales rep, you need to consider your value also.

If there were a star rating system for medical device sales, would you be worthy of even one, or maybe, two or three stars? How do you measure yourself? Do you have any kind of a rating system that you examine yourself with on a regular basis… daily, weekly, monthly, yearly?

Here are some areas you should consider in evaluating yourself:

✓ **Do you provide service that meets a consistently high standard?**

✓ **Is your service timely, organized and constantly above and beyond the call of duty?**

✓ **Does your knowledge and expertise provide valuable insight to your customers?**

✓ **Will your customers appreciate your service enough to tell their colleagues about you?**

You see, it doesn't matter what type of product you sell - the principles remain the same. What matters is the value you add to the product for the patient, the surgeon, and the hospital. In fact, you may even influence surgical advancement as a whole. This is what will distinguish you from your competitors and your colleagues.

Compare yourself to the other sales reps in your area. They are your control group - forget about those you don't know. There is no way to compare yourself to the unknown. You just need to be teh best rep in your area. Think about the concrete. Do your customers see you as the smartest and ultimately the best rep around?

There are so many different dynamics in our industry, you must absolutely be the best sales rep in your territory to win the prize.

Goal 1: Be The Best Medical Device Rep In Your Territory

In the Dreamworks SKG animated film Madagascar, Marty the zebra is standing in a herd of his fellow zebras when he suddenly comes to the realization...he is not recognizable. He looks like all the other zebras. He doesn't stand out.

For a zebra, that's probably a good thing. But for a sales rep? That's death.

Now, take a mental snapshot of yourself standing

amongst your colleagues and competition. Do you stand out? Or are you just like Marty?

What are the things that you do differently...or better? (Write them down)

1._____

2._____

3._____

Knowing your purpose is all-important. After all, you are taking up the doctor's valuable time. In the operating room, you are a potential source of infection. For you to be seen as valuable, fulfilling your purpose must outweigh everything else.

Can you articulate your purpose in the big scheme of things? If you can't, what value do you bring your customer?

Why are you in the OR? (Write down your purpose.)

1._____

2._____

Now let's examine your value proposition. The valuable medical device sales rep is the successful one. What makes him valuable is being a true consultant. He or she brings valuable knowledge to the surgeon for the patient's benefit.

The sales rep's knowledge may also benefit future

patients by helping to advance the field of surgery. The successful consultative medical device sales rep stands out from the competition because of the service he or she provides to the greater good of all concerned.

In what areas of medical device sales does such a consultant thrive?

Medical Device Salaries

Opportunities in our business are plentiful. The industry is moving at light speed, in both product innovation and sales innovation. The complacent sales rep is an easy target for the competition to pick off. He or she probably relies on tenuous

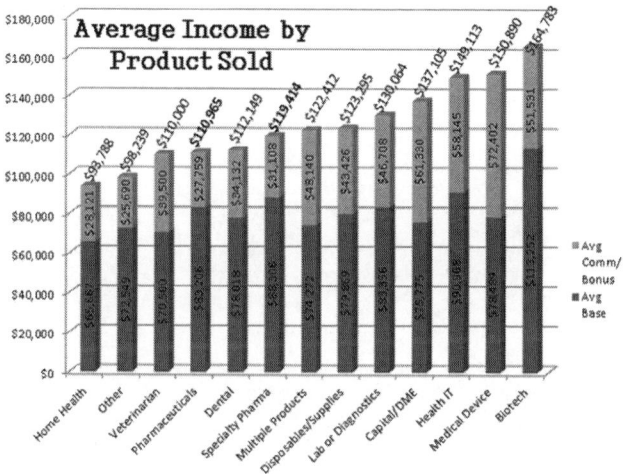

relationships with surgeons to make most sales. But these relationships are quickly losing value, as purchasing decisions are now being made less by surgeons and more by hospital administrators. In Chapter 3, we will discuss building relationships with the new major decision-makers: Value Analysis Committees (VAC).

For now, if you are feeling complacent, get over it quickly. If you aren't, go get the complacent rep's business. It's there for the picking.

Today's medical device sale is in flux. The surgeon-sales rep relationship is still a component, yes, but healthcare dynamics have changed the customer's preference power. Price bundling and IDN agreements are a factor. Contracting is changing too and remains a mobile target. In this period of uncertainty, a thorough understanding of a hospital's needs and a creative solution is required.

In his 2013 *Harvard Business Review* article, "Escaping the Discount Trap," Eric T. Anderson tells a poignant story of a Brazilian medical device sales company at a crossroads. The company can continue selling at discounted prices to its longtime customer, a charity-funded hospital which claims to have influence with other customers in the region… or it can make a stand to avoid falling into the price erosion trap.

The rep in this scenario got pinched on price, but came to his customer with a solution to increase the number of patients driven to the practice. The solution was to provide affordable blood pressure cuffs to rural patients, in order to diagnose high blood pressure. The rep sold more and the doctor developed more patients. Now that's consultative selling.

How to get the hospital to prioritize value over price? The key is to convince the customer that solution-based sales and pricing, utilizing the sales team as consultants, is beneficial both for their bottom line and for the patients.

In this case, as in all medical device sales in a cost-averse market, creativity and strategy are vital. A situation like the one described above could take months of planning and preparation before an actual sales call.

Selling now is more subtle. It requires a different mindset, but the resources are available. Most companies have the skills in-house to provide value-based pricing or solution-based selling to the customer.

First, find out:

✓ **Where the customer's greatest need lies**

✓ **Why the customer is buying...from you or from your competitor**

✓ **How you can help your customer understand your unique value proposition**

While opportunities in medical device sales are abundant, the under-achieving sales rep is becoming obsolete. You don't have to work hard. Just work smart. If you outsmart your competition with strategy, creativity and confidence, you will have success.

Using the above three questions, let's explore some of our favorite words...words we will repeat often. Consider them your mantra for success.

Strategize: Know why your customer has selected you or your competitor for its medical device needs in the past. Use this information to strategize and plan your approach for your next sale.

Prepare: Prepare your sales program to fulfill your customer's needs. An academic hospital has different needs than a community-based hospital. Ensure that the outcomes addressed in your proposal directly touch on those particular needs. A hospital that is cost-averse wants to know the bottom line. So, prove your solution doesn't cost more, may cost less in the final analysis, or may even pay for itself. All this may be true, even if your product is more expensive when viewed by itself.

Stay Proactive: Hopefully you wouldn't wake up the morning of a major car trip and then decide which route to take. Likewise, ensure you have a plan to get from A to B before you need it. Roads change and conditions change. So do customer needs. In fact, who's making the decisions may change. Be sure you know what lies down the road. Building your own dynamic road map will prepare you in advance and keep you proactive.

Staying ahead of the curve

Today, more and more surgeons are employed by the hospital. Many factors, like bundled payments, ACOs, IDNs, evidence-based medicine and purchasing groups are all affecting healthcare. Our political environment adds to the uncertainty. Hospitals are nervous, uncertain about their futures as they see others "going out of business."

Medicare now penalizes surgeons and hospitals for poor outcomes. Accountability is high. While this accountability makes hospitals nervous, it gives you an opportunity to prove your worth as a consultant.

Steer your surgeons toward procedures like MIS. There is value in less blood loss, lower infection rates, length of stay, and so on.

Now let's look at the playing field. Let's get to know our market.

What is the role of the sales rep in the patient care continuum?

You, the Sales Professional: In order to fulfill your potential as a professional sales rep, you must know yourself. Understand your inherent qualities, attributes and challenges. There is no longer a typical personality type that is best at sales. Maybe there never was. The days of the traditional extrovert, hard-selling, door-to-door salesman are long gone. The techniques that moved Encyclopedia Britannica, Electrolux, Fuller Brush and others don't do so well these days.

New, innovative sales methods are being adopted now. Amazon and Netflix, for example, understand creative selling which actually fulfills customer needs is what brings success.

Uber has increased the pool of available drivers by use of innovative softward, disrupting the market and taking share. Also they are adjusting price, based on demand, which we see restaurants and other businesses following.

Coffee Is For Closers?

One of the most famous scenes in the movie *Glengarry Glen Ross* features Alec Baldwin's character schooling the mopey salesman played by Jack Lemmon on the ABC's of selling: "Always...Be...Closing!"

But today's customers don't want to be "closed." Especially the sophisticated, knowledgeable ones. A hard sell followed by a hard close will most likely turn off most people. Gentle influence and subtle but credible persuasion based on factual evidence is more effective.

Personality Type and the Art of the Sale

In today's consultative sales process, you are a partner to your customer. You assist them to achieve the best possible outcome for their patients. An introvert can do this just as easily as an extrovert.

Do you know your personality type? Knowing

yourself well helps build the sales strategy that works best for you.

The Myers-Briggs Type Indicator (MBTI) is an excellent way to discover your personality traits. It is a psychometric assessment tool that helps determine how individuals perceive reality and make decisions. It is based on theories by noted psychologist Carl Jung, as published in his 1921 book.

The original MBTI was created by Katharine Cook Briggs and her daughter, Isabel Briggs Myers. They began developing the assessment during World War II, as a tool to help women entering the workforce for the first time. It helped identify jobs where they would be "most comfortable and effective."

Who is an introvert and who is an extrovert?

An introvert is someone who is energized by spending time alone. While introverts are often thought of as shy, this is not always the case. It simply means that after spending time in crowds or at social functions, introverts may need time alone to recharge their batteries.

An extrovert, on the other hand, is someone who thrives on the energy of group interaction. He or she would choose a party or social gathering over what they would consider less rewarding time spent alone.

Extroverts were traditionally assumed to perform better in careers that involved sales. They were thought to be better at engaging in conversations, sharing enthusiasm and persuading others about their product or service. Ultimately they were seen to be better at controlling a propect's behavior and obtaining a sale.

What about the ambivert?

Believe it or not, modern research has shown that extroverts are not statistically better at sales. A study by Wharton School of Business' Adam Grant identified another type of personality he calls the ambivert. This is an individual who has a balance of extroverted and introverted features. He or she is moderately comfortable in groups, but also craves time alone.

Grant looked at extroversion and introversion as a spectrum. He found that those who were highly introverted or highly extroverted did not perform as well as those who were closer to the middle. His findings clearly showed that ambiverts, whether closer to the introverted or extroverted sides of the middle, performed the best at sales.

Grant's research shows almost anyone can excel at sales. If you are intuitive enough to read your customer and tone down any excessive introverted or extroverted traits when necessary, you can succeed. Knowing yourself and your personality helps you understand how to make your customer as comfortable with you as possible.

Your Customer's Personality

Understanding your customer and his or her needs is critical to success in sales. Responding to your customer's personality gives you knowledge about them. In sales, as in life, knowledge is power.

Sales Tips for All Types of Personalities

✓ Mimic your customers

✓ Be an active listener

✓ Always come across as positive and non-confrontational

✓ Ask open-ended questions rather than making statements, reinforcing the consultative nature of your relationship

✓ Use interrogative self-talk to prepare for sales calls. Use "Can I do it?" questions instead of "I can do it" statements. This actually increases your effectiveness by 50%

Read these books to gain more insight into how to improve your selling:

Marilee Adams, *Change Your Questions, Change Your Life: 10 Powerful Tools for Life and Work*

Daniel H. Pink, *To Sell Is Human: The Surprising Truth About Moving Others*

CHAPTER SUMMARY

• **A successful sales rep is an expert in consultative sales. He or she acts as a colleague to the customer, a professional who makes the doctor better by providing the best tools and the best practices for their use.**

- **Hold yourself to the highest standards of practice. Devise a rating system for yourself to regularly evaluate your performance.**

- **Strategize and plan to be ahead of the curve.**

- **Don't focus on your close. Focus on the process of influence and persuasion.**

- **Find a sales style that is comfortable, natural, believable and persuasive, by knowing your personal strengths and challenges.**

Chapter 1 Endnotes

[1] Anderson, ET. "Escaping the Discount Trap," *Harvard Business Review,* Sep 2013.

[2] Daniel H. Pink, *To Sell Is Human: The Surprising Truth About Moving Others*

[3] Carl Jung, *Psychological Types*, 1923

[4] Barrick, M. R., Mount, M. K., & Judge, T. A. (2001) "Personality and performance at the beginning of the new millennium: What do we know and where do we go next?" *International Journal of Selection and Assessment,* 9, 9–30.

[5] Adam M Grant, "Rethinking the Extraverted Sales Ideal: The Ambivert Advantage," *Psychological Science,* 24(6) 1024 –1030

Chapter 2

The Science of Sales

Training and Practicing

Over our years in the medical device industry, we have hired many sales reps. Some have been great and some have been not so great. After working with and getting to know so many, we have identified these important attributes that seem to exist in every successful sales rep.

These winning characteristics are:

• Clinically and technically sound practices

• Solid work ethic and drive

• Intellectual curiosity and dynamic ability to learn

• Strong sales acumen

Each of the above attributes can be learned and improved. Some aspects of sales acumen may be more difficult for some people to grasp, but we have successfully taught many motivated sales reps how to improve in all these areas.

Let's start by looking at what you need to know.

The 3 Keys to a Sound Sales Rep

A good medical device sales rep has a thorough understanding of three areas of knowledge...

Clinical

✓ Anatomy

✓ Pathophysiology

✓ Radiology/Diagnostics

✓ Treatments/Procedures

Technical

✓ Product

✓ Inventory

Sales

How do you acquire all the above knowledge… especially if you have just started in the life sciences field or in a new specialty? The answer is simple, but not easy. You have to apply yourself to each one, until you can speak comfortably with anyone you contact.

Clinical - Anatomy, Physiology, Diagnostics, Treatments

Knowing how the human body works is essential to being a good medical device sales rep. This also applies to the life sciences arena. If you know the body, you can more easily handle objections. If you aren't secure in your knowledge of the body, bite the bullet and take a course.

Your colleagues may be able to direct you to appropriate resources or you can do some research online. If you are doing self-study, be sure you have some way to evaluate yourself, so you can measure your broadened knowledge base.

Netter's Anatomy is a great book to have. I personally keep color copies of the pages I find most important in my briefcase to reference them periodically.

Examples of other good books:

- *Handbook of Fractures* - Egol and Koval

- *Spine Secrets* - Devlin

- *Handbook of Neurosurgery* - Greenberg

- *Atlas of Human Anatomy* - Netter

- *Orthopedic Imaging* - Greenspan

- *Tarascon Pocket Orthopaedica* - Rispoli

- *Cardiology Essentials* - Teresa Holler

Knowledge about your specialty - "News Desk"

Knowledge is the key to becoming a real consultative sales expert. You should always have something new and interesting to share with your customers. It could be about what key opinion leaders are doing, industry developments, or a recap of a newly published paper. You can actually be your customer's news desk – their information curator – and establish yourself as an expert. Just make sure the news you deliver is relevant and not just gossip.

John's Tip!

How do you become well read quickly? You can't. But you can get started now, building up your knowledge over time. Every day you'll know a little more. Pick a journal to start with, the most prestigious specific to your specialty. (For example, the New England Journal of Medicine would probably be too general, though it should also be on your reading list.)

Then, read the introduction and abstract of every single article, every single month. The article is summarized in the abstract, but when you are getting started, the introduction may be even more important. It helps you understand the kinds of questions and answers your customers want. It usually quotes multiple authors and previous studies, providing an excellent background and history in the specialty.

Then, when you see your doctor, ask something like: "Have you read the latest article on...." Or, "I was looking through an old Journal article and it said.... do you agree with that?" Ask questions like, "Is that the right methodology?" and so on.

Once you better understand your physician's thought process and treatment options, you can better align your products and offering to meet specific needs he or she may have. This ultimately increases the value you bring. Soon, you will be viewed more as a colleague or a consultant than a sales rep.

An excellent source of the latest knowledge in your specialty is Google Scholar. This tool helps you quickly access articles, often even the full version, free of charge. It's also an easy way to find out what your surgeon has written – and you absolutely MUST know that.

Go ahead and try it right now. Search your two top customers on Google Scholar. What did you find? How can you reposition one of your products to take advantage of your new knowledge?

Write it down here: _____

_____

In addition, you'll find it is very helpful to...

• Understand how your doctors evaluate a patient for a given procedure or diagnosis.

• Know what key elements in a patient's history, physical exam and diagnosis determine when to use a given product.

• Master the diagnostic tools: lab values, radiographs, MRI, CT, Ultrasound, EMG, Echo, etc.

• Be aware of why your customer's referring docs are sending them patients. Hint: there may be an opportunity to add value here.

• Ask to do a preceptorship (ride-along) with your surgeon in their clinic. Only ask for a half-day. Pick a morning, when they're fresh and ahead of schedule.

Technical - Product and Inventory

We are including this short section because Product and Inventory are on the list of technical knowledge you should have, but these are obvious. With an intelligent, well-educated, professional customer base, you can't just fly by the seat of your pants. You won't sell them something you don't know intimately.

Your company probably provides you plenty of training, support, material, and more. Read everything. Learn everything. Know everything. This is typically something medical device companies do a good job with. Remember, your only value in the OR/Suite is your expertise on the product. That's why you're there, not to play comedian or DJ.

Sales

This is the most difficult to define of the above 3 keys. You may intellectually know about sales, but how can you know if you're actually putting your knowledge into practice? And what about that vague concept of Sales Acumen? Do you have it? How do you know? How can you measure it?

Before we answer those questions, we need to understand what we are trying to assess.

We define Sales Acumen as: an intuitive understanding of customer needs (they may not know what they need) with a subtle sense of how to approach the sale.

Sales Acumen can be innate with some people, but it can also be easily acquired. It's all about understanding your company and understanding your customer. Below is a definition of Sales Acumen from another publication.

A Sales Rep with Sales Acumen:

1. Is Self Motivated

2. Builds Relationships

3. Understands Unspoken Objections

4. Handles Rejection

(*Small Business,* "What Is a Sales Acumen?," by Carol Deeb)

You can understand your expected sales cycle by looking at the number of visits it takes to close a sale and what happens during each of those meetings. Often surgeons will look to a good sales consultant to provide real time updates and knowledge of their industry.

If you are up-to-date on your specialty and have mastered consultative selling techniques, this is easy. As noted above, it does require motivating yourself and building relationships, as well as understanding objections and even bouncing back from rejection.

Now, here are some basic questions to ask yourself about your Sales Acumen. Fill in the answers on the space provided. (Again, please write in this book.)

1. How long does it typically take you to get your first scheduled appointment with a new doctor?

_____

2. How many sales calls/touch points does it take you to get new business? And consistent business?

_____

3. How many cold calls are you doing in a week? And in a month?

_____

4. Are you proactively engaging with everyone in the sales cycle? (Patient, Hospital, Doctor - PHD)

_____

5. Do you spend time pre-planning your sales calls on a daily and weekly basis? How much time?

_____

6. How often do you role-play or practice your sales calls?

_____

Answering these questions helps you understand your current work ethic, motivation and mastery of consultative selling. More important, it shows how you need to prioritize your time in order to grow your business.

Be sensitive to the individual styles of your customers. As described in *Integrity Selling Process* by Ron Willingham, they may be classified as a Talker, Doer, Supporter or Controller. Find ways to provide information to them in different ways amenable to their style. Some will want journal articles. Others will want to hear about current events. Some just want you to tell them about new procedures or techniques and what their peers are doing. Deliver what they want. Be more valuable to them than your competitor is.

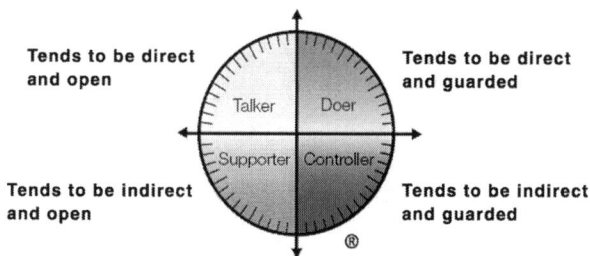

Provide information for your customers' personal interests as well as their professional. You may know your surgeon likes fishing or football. This doesn't mean you should invite him for a weekend at your uncle's fishing cabin, but he might enjoy hearing about the scouting report on a new draft pick for his favorite football team. Stay alert for opportunities to connect.

Finally, Sales Acumen also has a social and cultural component. Your customers are highly educated individuals with plenty of disposable income and a cultured lifestyle. Ensure that you have strong social skills, a good handshake, exquisite table manners, and basic food and wine appreciation.

Develop a well-rounded knowledge of music, art, travel, sports, and current affairs. One would think all this goes without saying, but often people ignore or forget obvious things. For example, did you know... you always pass the salt with the pepper, never just one or the other? And so on...

Selling a New Procedure

When you're selling a new procedure, you are in uncharted territory. Every customer is a new customer. Every sales call is a chance to refine your pitch. Take this new procedure as an opportunity. You will be making a lot of calls, so you can become an expert. Many times you see senior sales reps resist change.

For example, when Nuvasive introduced XLIF (lumbar spine fusion technique), spine reps with experience typically didn't do well. So Nuvasive hired reps with little knowledge of the spine hardware industry. To sell something innovative, they needed to avoid older reps' preconceived notions about the traditional marketplace. As a result, NuVasive sales rep training became one of the most comprehensive and respected in the industry.

Before you go out on new procedure sales calls, it is critical that you are prepared and organized. Remember, planning and preparation are the keys to your success. There may be kinks to be worked out Don't just be a guinea pig with new products and procedures. Be the experimenter.

Speak to other reps who have dealt with this new device, whether they're in Marketing, Specialty Sales or Alpha Release. Find out all of the objections they have faced and how they handled them. Also remember, the collateral with these products may not be completely up to date.

You are going to need to know everything about your procedure before you go into the field. This is the time to really dig into those company resources.

Before you visit your first customer, understand everything below about the products in your bag.

1. The limitations of the procedure you are selling.

2. The pros and cons associated with your procedure. Brainstorm with co-workers to prepare for common objections.

3. The risks of complication. How they are different from prior techniques or procedures for this pathology.

4. How your doctor might treat new complications.

5. The learning curve. Data and success stories from other clinicians. This should include:

a. How many cases your customer will consider a fair trial? Ask for this number of cases upfront!

b. How many cases they will need to feel comfortable?

c. How many cases it will take before they are working at optimal efficiency?

6. New techniques are associated with increased complication rates. You must know and convey to your customer that initial results may be less than desirable. This may include longer procedure times, possibly increased blood loss, and a staff not completely "in synch," among other difficulties. Encourage your surgeons to start with easier pathologies and indications when adopting a new technique.

7. Lab Time, Demo Set Practice, Sawbones, Animations. The best way to have a positive outcome in your first case is to have struggled with the product yourself.

8. BE THE EXPERT - If your surgeon senses uncertainty with you about the procedure, that's a good reason for him to refuse it or to go with another company.

In-servicing is invaluable. On first time cases, it's a MUST.

Despite all these complications, you can sell a new procedure effectively. As always, it just takes preparation and planning, focusing on the benefits of the new procedure regarding pathology and indications. A good, open-minded sales strategy aligns the new procedure's clinical basis with the problems of conventional techniques.

CHAPTER SUMMARY- 3 Keys

• **There are 3 key areas of knowledge essential to any clinically sound sales rep: Clinical, Technical and Sales.**

• **Knowledge of human anatomy and physiology is important, along with specialty-specific knowledge. If you aren't an expert, sign up for a course and subscribe to important journals in your field.**

• **Build your sales acumen by deepening your understanding of your customer's sales cycle and ensuring you have the social graces to be comfortable with your customer in any setting.**

CHAPTER SUMMARY- For New Products

• **Selling a new procedure takes much more preparation than an old one.**

• **Embrace this opportunity.**

• **Understand as many objections as you can before you head out on your first call.**

• **Know the risks, limitations, and learning curve for the average surgeon.**

• Base your sales call on the pathology and indications addressed by the new procedure and compare it with conventional techniques.

• Don't just be a guinea pig. Do your homework. Find out what challenges others have encountered. You only get one shot to make a first impression.

Chapter 2 Endnotes

[1] http://scholar.google.com/intl/en/scholar/about.html

Integrity Selling Process, Ron Willingham

Netter's Anatomy

(Small Business, "What Is a Sales Acumen?" Carol Deeb

Chapter 3

Know Your Market: Who Are Your Customers?

The PHDs

Before you can develop a strategy and devise a plan, you must understand your customer. Your market is actually made up of a number of players who all influence your sales. We call them the "PHDs." (Patients, Hospitals, Doctors)

Who are the decision makers?

Decisions about medical device purchases and procedures used to be made exclusively by the doctor. This is no longer true. The term "Physician Preference Item" is dying!

While this has changed the selling landscape, you can still maintain control over your sales process and account. Many sales reps tend to rely on someone else to manage these relationships. For example, they might let corporate deal with hospital compliance contracts. Don't you do that. You need to be the manager of your account. You can steer each decision-making point for each of the players In the selling scenario.

The Patient

A patient makes a number of choices before deciding to have an elective surgical procedure. Among the questions they ask are the following:

Should I have the surgery?

- Which surgeon should I choose?

- Which implant do I want? (Many devices and procedures are now advertised directly to patients.)

- Do I know anyone who has experienced this procedure and/or this surgeon?

- Which facility will I be most comfortable with? Which has the best reputation? (Hospitals specialize in specific departments and market them accordingly, such as, "Cardio/Ortho Center of Excellence.")

- Does this surgeon perform XYZ procedure that I read about on the Internet? (For example, a Laser Spine Procedure, Gastric Bypass, or Cardio Ablation.)

Patients will also usually ask the surgeon many specific questions about the given procedure and the recovery process. Surgeons complain about misinformed patients who arrive armed with information from Google or WebMD, hoping to have minimally invasive surgical (MIS) procedures. They need to be able respond to these patients. After all, elective surgeons also have to run a business and make sales, just as we do.

So, consider what tools and materials you can provide to help the surgeon reassure patients. Be creative in your thinking! There are compliant ways to help. See the TIPS AND TRICKS section for specific ways to do so.

TIPS AND TRICKS

✓ Referrals from other patients

✓ Referrals from nursing homes and physical therapy

✓ Marketing collateral aimed at patients and the community: brochures, billboards, commercials, magazines, etc. Hopefully your company does this.

✓ Educational dinners where doctors meet doctors

✓ Specialist talks to primary care docs to attract more patients

✓ Hospitals may market specialty departments and centers of excellence, such as robotics, navigation, MIS surgery, etc.

✓ Company-sponsored educational links your surgeons can use on their websites.

The Hospital

Ray's Story

Two days a week, I would arrive at my local hospital parking lot in scrubs, ready for a day in the OR with my

surgeon. I would always be one of the first cars in the lot. Without fail, a gentleman in a fancy suit, driving a Lexus would arrive at the same time. We began nodding hello to each other. Some months in, I pointed him out to someone and asked who he was. It turned out he was the hospital CEO and his name was Kevin.

From that day forward, I began greeting him with, "Hey, Kevin, how are you?" Over the course of two years he watched my diligent early arrival and returned my friendly greeting week after week. We would walk into the hospital together and part ways. I would go right to the OR and he would go left to the administrative suites. We often crossed paths in the hallways and cafeteria during the day, always acknowledging each other.

Then one day I found myself in a meeting with the OR director and the purchasing manager for a price negotiation...in Kevin's office...with Kevin. When I arrived, Kevin almost jumped out of his chair to welcome me. He then proceeded to tell the others how diligent and professional I was. Before that day, he had had no idea what my role in the hospital was, but I had made a positive impression just by my punctuality and friendliness.

I received a limited vendorship as a result of that meeting and Kevin strongly supported me to continue doing business with his hospital.

What does this story tell us? Know the C-Suite in the hospital and treat everyone with a hospital badge equally. There are hidden decision-makers, influencers, and gatekeepers everywhere. Let's examine some steps to achieving success within the hospital.

Step One: Determine who the decision makers are. This may take time, listening and finesse. Do not just assume it is the supply chain coordinator. The people you're looking for may be OR suite coordinators, nurse managers, SPD technicians or inventory coordinators. Every facility has a different political structure, whether explicit or hidden.

Today, it is easier than ever to find out who a hospital CEO or CFO is by simply going to the hospital website. It's amazing what you can learn from the CEO's bio/profile. Become familiar with names of the leaders and include this info on your customer profile.

Who are the CEOs of your two top accounts?

1._____

2._____

Step Two: Master the process of adding products to your facility: be proactive. You may not always need surgeon or healthcare professional support. Understand the paperwork required for additional product listings. Is there a committee that okay's each addition? Who is on that committee?

Before you even start the process of adding a new product, have your pricing dialed in. You do not want to delay acceptance by having to go back and ask for pricing parameters. Then, always give the decision makers more than they ask for. Remember all 10 elements of review. (Listed below.) Include essential tools for success like routed clinical papers to support the use of your device, as well as all the marketing literature and tools available. (Think digital.)

The Decision Maker: The VAC (Value Analysis Committee)

This is now the new trend across the US. Most hospitals are moving toward assembling this kind of committee.

A publication in *Boston Healthcare*, October, 2013, "Articulating the Value Proposition of Innovative Medical Technologies in the Healthcare Reform Landscape," details this quite well.

10 Key Elements Of A VAC Review:

1. Revenue Impact
2. Return On Investment
3. Complication Rate
4. Accuracy
5. Safety
6. OR Turnaround
7. Ease of Use
8. Price
9. Patient Outcomes
10. Length of Stay

Make-Up Of This Committee:

- Clinicians
- Nursing

- Risk Management
- Finance
- C-Suite

Tip: Price is only one of 10 factors! Position your product properly the first time with the VAC and you may be able to hold price.

Be in control of your account. While the decision-making power may be moving away from those you touch on a daily basis, you still need to stay on top of your account. We regularly see sales reps who don't know when their customers' contracts are expiring or even which products are under contract. This basic, easily-obtainable information is vital. Just because a contract exists doesn't mean you should leave everything up to the corporate contracting department.

When are your two top accounts' contracts expiring?

1._____

2._____

Who is your purchasing/procurement manager at your top account? When was the last time you visited them just to say hi, with no agenda?

The Doctor/Healthcare Provider (HCP)

In today's landscape, hospitals are buying up other hospitals, as well as private medical and surgical practices. Surgeons are increasingly becoming hospital employees.

When a hospital system owns a practice, the doctor loses a lot of decision-making power on implants. He or she may still influence decisions, but no longer make them. Depending on the hospital's contractual obligations, the surgeon may now only have a choice between two competing implants.

One very important point you need to always consider: what benefits do the surgeon and the hospital have in common? This makes doing business easy and expedites your execution. Stress those benefits. How do you add value to make your product align with these benefits? Do you know what the RVU's or reimbursement are for your surgeon? How about the reimbursement for the facility?

Ten years ago, things were very different. A doctor could simply demand an implant from a hospital or threaten to take his patient load to another facility. Today, that power is gone, but the doctor's responsibility still remains. The end user, the surgeon, takes on all the responsibility for using a particular device. He or she is responsible for all failures, complications and mortality...essentially all the decisions that take place in the OR.

	All	Gender		Age		
		Women	Men	Under 40	40 to 54	55+
Ownership status						
Owner	53.2%	38.7%	59.6% [a]	43.3%	51.4% [a]	60.0% [a]
Employee	41.8%	55.7%	35.8% [a]	51.3%	44.2% [a]	34.7% [a]
Independent contractor	5.0%	5.7%	4.7%	5.4%	4.5%	5.3%
	100%	100%	100%	100%	100%	100%
Type of practice						
Solo practice	18.4%	21.0%	17.3% [a]	10.0%	15.8% [a]	25.3% [a]
Single specialty group	45.5%	39.7%	48.0% [a]	46.2%	46.7%	43.8%
Multi-specialty group	22.1%	23.0%	21.6%	27.0%	21.6% [a]	20.3% [a]
Direct hospital employee	5.6%	5.7%	5.6%	9.3%	6.3% [b]	3.1% [a]
Faculty practice plan	2.7%	2.3%	2.9%	2.4%	3.4%	2.2%
Other [2]	5.7%	8.2%	4.6% [a]	5.2%	6.3%	5.3%
	100%	100%	100%	100%	100%	100%
N	3466	976	2490	724	1747	995

Source: AMA 2012 Physician Practice Benchmark Survey.

Comment: The data from the table above shows that today physicians work in a wide variety of practice settings. Notably, fewer physicians are owners of their practice. In 2012, 53% of physicians owned their practice, a drop of 8% since 2007/2008. Only 18.4% remained in solo practice, down from 24% in 2007/2008. Most telling, 42% of physicians were employees in 2012.

Consider the physician's heavy responsibility, coupled with limited decision-making power. It's a precarious position. In order for you, the sales rep, to manage the doctor, you must understand that responsibility and how he or she came to have it.

Understanding Your Customer's Personality, Background and Training

There are typically four personality types of

surgeons. In order to best serve them and sell them, you need to understand who they are and what motivates them. Below are the four major types, but don't forget, some doctors may be hybrids of more than one type.

To begin, ask yourself and others is this a surgeon who:

1) Likes the podium?
2) Likes great service?
3) Has financial interests?
4) Values their relationships?

If a surgeon likes the podium, you can help them get there. If they like great service, you can provide that. If your surgeon is moved mostly by money, help them understand how your implant will attract more patients and grow their practice. If they value relationships, make sure you fulfill yours with attention and integrity.

Once you know what motivates your surgeon, find out about their background and training. The best sales reps have an intimate understanding of what it takes to be a surgeon or healthcare professional in their specialty. Understanding the schooling and training your customers go through will help you relate to them. Understanding the subtle nuances of training from various programs provides even more insight.

For example, some programs provide hands-on training from the first day of residency, while others keep residents from touching patients until they have a couple of years of observation under their belts. Don't be afraid to ask. Most surgeons are happy to talk about their training and this gives you more in common.

Know where and how your surgeon was trained. This provides insight into who has influenced them and why they do what they do. If they used a given system in training, they are more likely to continue that system in practice. Armed with this information, you can now quickly and efficiently convert the business. We will discuss this further in the Family Tree section of Chapter 4.

We understand learning all this information is not easy. There are so many sub-specialties, it would be impossible for us to list them all here. If you want to look up how your surgeon may have been trained, you can start by visiting www.acgme.org

Examples of typical training programs

General Surgeon:

- Undergrad
- 4 years of Medical School, either MD or DO
- 5 years of General Surgeon Residency

Orthopedic Surgeon (Non Specialized):

- Undergrad - 4years of Medical School, either MD or DO
- 5 years of Orthopedic Residency

Orthopedic Surgeon (Sports Medicine):

- Same as above, plus 1 year of Fellowship

Cardiothoracic Surgeon:

- Undergrad
- 4 years of Medical School, either MD or DO
- 5 years of General Surgeon Residency + 2-3 years of fellowship

Physician Assistant:

- Undergrad
- 2-3 years of Medical School training - most are Masters Programs

Nurse Practitioner:

- Undergrad in Nursing (BSN)
- 2 years of Grad School in Nursing

Registered Nurse:

- Either Associate's Degree or Bachelor's of Science in Nursing

Nurse Anesthetist:

- Undergrad in Nursing (BSN)
- 3 years of grad school with heavy clinical focus

Listening to the Customer

A guy walks into a clothing store. The salesperson asks, "How can I help you sir?" The guy responds that he is looking for a suit.

"This is a great suit and it's on sale," says the salesperson, showing him a light grey suit. The customer suggests that he would like something darker.

The salesperson proceeds to explain very persuasively that it's summer now, lighter colors are better for the season, and there's a full rack on sale right now.

The customer shakes his head and moves toward the door. As he is walking out, the manager sees him and asks, "Sir, did we not have what you want?"

The customer responds glumly, "I need a suit for my dad's funeral. I want a dark suit, but all the salesperson wanted to show me were light colors."

This story is an illustration of assumptions blotting out customer needs. The salesperson assumed the customer was: a) looking for a deal and b) interested in seasonal trends. If he had listened to what the customer was saying and followed up with the appropriate questions, he could have easily closed the sale and perhaps even made a friend in the process for future business.

Hear what your customer says. More important, be sure you really understand what they mean. Don't be afraid to ask questions.

Planning and Executing a Strategy

"Proper planning and preparation prevents piss-poor performance." The 7 "P's" of the British Military

Without an overall strategic plan, your sales call

is a one-off hit or miss. With it, every minute has a purpose and leads you in one direction or another. Based on scenarios you have mapped out ahead of time, you can know which way you are heading. Personalize your strategy for each of your customers by creating a game plan.

A football team has a strategy for the season, which they follow when putting together their roster, their practice regimen, their playbook and much more. They also have a game plan, which they adapt and follow for each game with each individual opponent.

Do you know what your overall strategy is? Without it, you can't create your sales game plan. You have to think step by step what tactics you are going to use. You must know on which call and interaction you are going to insert which product.

We define a business strategy as a high-level plan to achieve one or more goals under various conditions of uncertainty. By its nature, a strategy may be difficult and uncomfortable. A strategy is broad in scope, with specific areas of focus that help form and direct the business plan.

Strategy is larger than a business plan. It is a broad concept that encompasses everything a business does to make money. It is how a business attracts customers and achieves its goals. Here is a common business strategy taken from an actual example:

Example - Facebook's Instagram Acquisition

Facebook changed the mobile scene overnight in 2012 by acquiring the photo-sharing startup, Instagram, for an unprecedented $1B. At the time Instagram had just 30 million users. Fast-forward to 2014: Instagram's user base had already shot past 150 million. It is now the dominant photo-sharing app on all mobile platforms. Most important, it attracts teens, who are leaving Facebook in droves as older people join it.

The Strategy - Cornering A Fledgling Market

Facebook's strategy in acquiring Instagram was to: a) corner the fledgling mobile image-sharing market, and b) hedge its bets for future growth. Facebook ensured itself a competitive advantage over Google, Microsoft, and other competitors in the social media market. That's good strategy.

Components of a Business Plan

The following should be defined as Hospital or Surgeon based:

✓ **Opportunity** - What is available

✓ **Environment** - Your competition, contracting, VAC

✓ **Goals** - Clear and specific milestones in gaining access to the customer, growing the account, etc.

✓ **Objectives** - Profit or volume of business

✓ Tactics/Action Items - Formal customer interactions, corporate resources required, specialist assistance, etc.

✓ Timeline - 30-60-90 days, to roadmap your progress

✓ Scorecard/Measurables - On a monthly and quarterly basis

We believe in using the SMART Goal technique. All goals should be: Specific, Measurable, Achievable, Relevant, and Time-bound.

Components of a Business Strategy

A Solid Strategy = Fear and Discomfort

✓ Mission Statement - overarching, timeless expression of your purpose

✓ Guiding Principles - enduring, passionate and distinctive core beliefs

✓ SWOT Analysis - Strengths, Weaknesses, Opportunities, Threats

✓ Strategies - umbrella methods you intend to use to reach your mission

✓ Action Items - specific statements detailing how the goal will be accomplished

✓ Scorecard - track your performance against monthly targets

All right, let's put this all together, staying with sports analogies...

Football Team Strategy - Starts in the offseason for a team. Say they want to create a run and gun offense. In order for that to work, they will need to recruit great receivers and a star QB. They will have to rewrite all the playbooks, drills, line techniques and more.

Football Team Game Plan - This includes the actual plays they will be running from week to week. It will change in response to the opponent they are facing. For example, does that team blitz or do they run more zone defense? This will be dynamic and can even change mid-game.

Pre-Call and Post-Call Planning: Building the Continuum

Here are some simple planning tools and techniques that will help you to customize your strategy into a plan for each of your prospective and existing customers.

Sales Calls Templates

Templates are great for delivering pertinent information. The risk is that you may sound rehearsed, like a routine memorized message. The best presentation sounds like you are engaging in a conversation.

On the next page is a handy list of essential information you need, so you can create a template to use in order to keep track of all your customers. That way, you'll always have all the relevant info at your fingertips.

Save a template like this in your phone or in whatever you use to stay organized

Customer Contact Info

Surgeon Name _____

DOB _____

Practice Name _____

Phone Number Office _____

Doctor's Cell _____

Address _____

Building # _____

City/State/Zip _____

Surgery Scheduler Name & Number_____

PA's, NP & Office Mgr _____

Other Office Staff _____

Hospitals with Privileges _____

Hospital and OR Staff _____

Surgery Days & Locations _____

Office Days & Locations _____

Respect

Build respectful communication into your plan. This elevates your professionalism in the eyes of customers and coworkers. You will be more respected as well. Treating everyone well is important, not to mention just good manners. We have actually seen scrub techs or nurses blackball a sales rep because the rep treated them with less respect than the doctor. In one instance, an arrogant comment from a sales rep to the scrub tech eventually got that sales rep suspended from the OR by the hospital administration. Ouch.

Make friends with the OR nurses, scrub techs and anesthesiologists. Scrub techs are among the best assets you can have. They can provide valuable insight on your customer's needs, wants and opinions. They can also promote your product for you when you are not around, if they are well-informed, well-respected and feel good about you.

One of the biggest barriers to a conversion can be winning over the techs. They can make your product look good or bad. Back to being proactive - meet with them before the call, to inservice them and build rapport with them.

Even other reps can be great allies in the operating room. In addition, educational breakfast and lunch meetings with the scheduler have also garnered success for both of us.

Post-Call Notes

It should go without saying that after each and every sales call, you make notes and review your call. The more detailed the notes, the better. Six months from now your company may launch a new product that better aligns with what your doctor was looking for. In addition, post-call notes help you evaluate your interaction and plan for the next call. Form good habits like this, to stay organized and on top of your game.   Take the time to fill in your customer profile template or family tree. It will assist you with your next interaction.

48

writing key words, phrases, and points I liked vs. ones I didn't like. This practice gave me better skills for the next call, to execute at an increasingly higher level.

===

Planning for Potential Failure

Plan for your potential failure before it happens. Predict the objections and be prepared to handle them. Use previous post-call notes with similar customers for ideas. Even write out the customer's rejection. It may sound funny, but it will force you to put yourself into the customer's head. And that's a good place to be. You may find out you don't know as much about your customer as you think you do. So do more research and background work before the actual call. That's how to be prepared.

===

Make It Count:

If you find you can't predict or handle potential objections, then you are not prepared for the call. Stop. Start over and dig deeper. Typically you only have one shot. Make it count.

===

Being proactive, planning, and preparing are themes that run throughout this book. Game-planning your strategy for each customer prepares you for whatever you come up against and results in the best possible outcome. It may seem like it takes a lot of time, but you are actually saving time - and making money - by reducing failed calls.

Accountability

So, how do you win this game? This is your
paycheck, your career. We have given you lots of
tips and tricks, but only you can turn them into sales.
You need to take all these points and execute them.
That's not easy. It takes self-motivation and self-
responsibility. Don't wait for your manager to kick
your butt or for your teammate to book the calls.
Hold yourself accountable for your own success or
failure. Kick your own butt!

Multiple Touches

The more times you "touch" or interact with your
customer, the more successful you will be. Multiple
touches increase your opportunity for a sale. The
more repetition and practice you get, the better
you become at delivering your message. The more
interactions you have, the more likely you are to
succeed.

Tip: First Impressions Are Everything

*"He wanted to look like a million bucks, because he was
negotiating millions of dollars..."*

Drew Rosenhaus, *A Shark Never Sleeps*

You only get one opportunity to make a first impression.
What is yours? Great eye contact? Solid handshake? What

is your opening line? Please think about this and rehearse it.

Dress The Part!

When you're not in the OR, change out of those old scrubs and put your suit on. Period. How can anyone take you seriously if you're wearing pajamas? When John worked at The Mayo Clinic, the rule was no scrubs in the clinic. If you were seen walking through the Gonda Building in scrubs, your boss would get an email. Why? Mayo is a world-class institution. They pride themselves on top-level service and professionalism. Act like a world-class rep.

CHAPTER SUMMARY

• PHDs influence decisions, whether they are the direct decision makers or not.

• Find out who the real decision makers are in your market. They aren't always the obvious individuals.

• Understand your customers, their background, their needs, and their motivation.

• Creating a plan for each customer based on your overall strategy prepares you for most any scenario.

• Listen carefully to your customer. You may be hearing what you expect instead of what they say. Don't assume. Ask questions.

- **Sales call templates help crystallize your message ahead of time.**

- **Post-call notes keep track of conversations and encourage you to evaluate your performance. Avoid future failure by role-playing future objections.**

- **Multiple touches give you more practice as well as better understanding of your customer, so you can find them the best solution.**

- **Accountability and first impressions are all up to you.**

Chapter 3 Endnotes

[1] AMA 2012 Physician Practice Benchmark Survey

Boston Healthcare, October, 2013 "Articulating the Value Proposition of Innovative Technologies in the Healthcare Reform Landscape"

Accreditation Council for Graduate Medical Education - www.ACGME.org

Chapter 4

The Sales Call

Playing the Game

We know you have to juggle multiple professional priorities, which often encroach on your personal time. Yet, we still encourage you to spend even more time educating and preparing yourself for that all-important sales call, when everything is on the line. Becoming more effective in your call actually saves you time overall. Getting it right the first time is a great time-saver.

The key to being more time-efficient is prioritizing properly. Consider how many minutes a day you actually spend with your customer, engaging in conversation that pushes the sales needle. In fact, consider all your time management regarding sales-related activities:

1) Obtaining The Minutes
2) Preparing For Your Minutes & Customer Profiling
3) Being A Valued Consultant
4) Calling On Your Teammates

Obtaining Minutes

Be proactive. A complacent rep is satisfied to just bump into customers throughout their hospital or clinic day. A proactive rep works to arrange a lunch meeting, pin down other specific meetings, and plan concrete agendas for those meetings. Focus on making your time in the hospital or clinic really count.

Ray's Tips and Tricks:

✓ When you meet with a scheduler to book a sales call or an office appointment, don't just book one. Book the next available appointment and also add a monthly follow-up appointment through the end of the year. That's being proactive and efficient. If the scheduler says no, just use your sales skills and charm to get it done. You are not going to convert business on one call. Schedule six to nine months of appointments.

✓ The early bird gets a tasty worm. Breakfast! Lunch and dinner may be big commitments, tough to get with a potential new customer. Plus, they mean entertaining a prospect for two to three hours. It's like dating. Speed dating is less of a commitment, easier to handle. Your customer feels the same way. Book a breakfast. Sell to your customer in the proper environment, not in the parking lot or the elevator. Use controlled meetings, where you have their undivided attention, like breakfast, sit-down meetings, and so on.

Let's track your time. How many minutes do you have in your week?

7am to 6pm = 11 hours x 5 = 55 hours total (plus, maybe a little on the weekend)

Now, break it down. (Seriously, write in the book here.)

Hours spent commuting per week_____

Hours spent ordering/restocking inventory_____

Hours spent covering cases_____

Hours spent submitting VAC or meeting with purchasing_____

Hours waiting for delays and cases to start_____

Hours online non-work related_____

Hours scheduling meetings with customers_____

Hours engaging with customers to grow sales_____

You get the point? You do have time left in your week to become more successful. Most frequently, we see huge amounts of time spent commuting and dealing with inventory. So here are the questions to ask yourself in order to become more time-efficient.

• How can I minimize time spent in my car?

• Can I use another form of transportation?

• Can I consolidate a majority of my inventory ordering for the week into one or two calls?

• Can I streamline my set turnover within SPD?

• Can I do my inventory management tasks outside in the hallway when or before the case is getting started? (Instead of flirting with the nursing staff)

• If a case is delayed, can I still make good use of my time? (Run across the street to the clinic and set up future sales calls? Review the newest Journal articles or marketing collateral? Inservice the nurses/techs in the room on my newest product?)

Every medical device industry is different. You know best which efficiencies you can implement, if you focus on doing so. Then you'll have more time to proactively meet customers and grow your business.

John's Tip:

Don't forget to schedule one-on-one time with the physician assistants, nurse practitioners or RNs in the clinic. All too often they are the ones making decisions about what goes into their patients.

Planning and Preparing for Your Minutes

Ask yourself: What training do you do on a regular basis to prepare yourself for those top-priority meetings with your surgeon?

Ray's College Football Experience

I would practice on the field 15 hours a week, plus spend time on film and strategy. Then I would travel for an entire day...all just to play about 60 minutes on Saturday. (30 minutes as a defensive player.) Oh, yeah, and we spent most of the summer and spring training for the next year, just to do it all over again. But our team's record of wins and losses came down to those 60 minutes. The question was: how did we turn preparation into performance when it mattered most?

That's why you have to prepare...so you can perform when everyone is keeping score.

If you aren't sure how much time you spend preparing (don't feel too bad, because most sales reps aren't), it's time to start collecting data. Keep track for a week.

Data collection: Hopefully after doing the exercise above, you found some extra time. Now, let's get specific on how these valuable new minutes can be put to good use. Start by answering the questions below, again right here in your book.

1. How many hours a week are you working?_____

2. How many hours a week are you actually making a sales call?_____

3. During each sales call, how many minutes are you actually talking business?_____

4. How many sales calls per week are you making?_____

Multiply the number of sales calls times the minutes spent talking business. Now you know how many minutes you're really in the game.

Looking at the total hours in your work-week, calculate the percentage of time you are actually growing your business.

MAKE THAT NUMBER BIGGER AND YOU WILL MAKE YOUR PAYCHECK BIGGER.

Simple, right?

When we actually did this exercise ourselves, we were surprised to find we spent far less time in actual sales interactions than we thought. We all have to spend a lot of time on travel, preparation and strategy to be ready for these vital sales calls. If you want to really shine during those precious minutes, take time management seriously. It's the key to closing more sales.

So you found some precious minutes!

Many of us in our industry consistently work 55 or more hours per week. Typically, we're doing well if 10% of that time is actually engaged with a decision maker trying to move mind-share. That would be five and a half hours a week. Even then, we spend less time in the actual act of selling.

There is a lot of set-up that goes into the sales

process and it's all-important. We could never make a sales call without the prep work: scheduling lunches, waiting in the OR, driving across town to catch a doctor at the end of the day.

So when you do get those vital few minutes to meet, how prepared are you? Have you done everything possible? Do you practice daily, so that when an opportunity suddenly presents itself, you are ready to perform?

Or do you freeze up and just regurgitate product knowledge?

Any engagement with a customer is a sales call. Get your point across! Your surgeon or healthcare provider doesn't need you to be buddies. Show them what they do need for their practrice and you'll have a good customer.

John Says:

When I was practicing medicine as a physician assistant, I saw between 5 and 10 sales reps each week. Some were medical device reps, others were pharmaceutical and durable medical equipment reps. All of them knew I was an ironman triathlete and a cyclist. Almost all of them invited me on a bike ride.

I had no interest in going for a ride with someone I didn't know. It was clear they were just trying to befriend me in order to sell me. I had plenty of real friends. I didn't want any fake ones. This ploy was obvious to me and it will be to your customers too, so be careful.

There are better ways to insert yourself in your customer's life. Make sure, if you invite customers to events, that they're appropriate and interesting. Time your ask properly and know a lot about your customers before you ask.

Ray's Tip:

Using an approved whitepaper of a journal article lets you take the conversation to a clinical perspective. Then you can explore the surgeon's beliefs and practice style. Ultimately you'll be able to align your value proposition with his needs.

Here are some habits you need to practice at least daily, to be prepared at all times:

• Make pre- and post-call notes on all your decision makers. Enter details of each healthcare provider into the contacts section of your phone. This should include personal information, like: interests, spouse's name, kids' names and approximate ages, plus any other info you have.

• Review your customer notes on a weekly basis to stay fresh. Many times, just reviewing this information may remind you of a sales technique that has worked in the past.

• Write out your sales call for all new products. This creates a concise, direct way of delivering your message. There is an awesome connection between your brain, your hands and your mouth. When you can collect your thoughts, put them on paper, and then edit them - your sales pitch is complete. You have organized everything you want to say. When the opportunity arises with a doctor, you can deliver your message clearly, coherently and charismatically.

• Role playing and practicing in the mirror are also useful. Focus on clarity and power. Don't be wordy. Short and concise is ALWAYS better. Your doctor is smarter than you think.

• Have questions ready that can get a sales call headed in the direction you want. It doesn't matter how the doctor answers. By getting those answers, you better understand how and why your customer makes buying decisions.

Customer Profiles

This is your proverbial "little black book." It's the sales rep's bible. You can keep it forever, no matter where you go in your career, with your present company or another. The more specific you are with your entries, the more valuable this tool becomes.

On the next two pages, we've given you all the possible information you need to create your own templates that you can use for your customer profiles.

Track your progress and you will increase it!

Surgeon Profile Info & Sales Notes - Pre & Post

Education_____

Fellowship_____

Residency_____

Medical School _____

Undergrad _____

Hometown _____

Family Information

Spouse's Name _____

Children's Names and Ages_____

_____

HobbieseActivities _____

_____

Favorite Sport and Sports Teams

_____

Community Involvement/Charities

_____

Type of Surgical Procedures Performed

_____

_____

Payer Mix (Insurance, Cash, Medicare, Medicaid)

_____

_____

What Products Are You Targeting _____

_____

_____

Assets Needed from Manager/Corporate

_____

Notes from Last interaction Date_____

_____

_____

Next Steps_____

_____

_____

Family Tree

This strategy has been tried and tested many times in our sales process. It is one of the most powerful tactics we know. It can accelerate a sales process remarkably, by connecting to a meaningful time in a doctor's life.

A doctor's "Family Tree" refers to the people he studied with during medical school, residency and fellowship. Ray compares this connection to one he knows well...meeting someone who knows anyone he played football with for four years in college. Those four years were some of the best times of his life, with some of the most indelible memories. Why? Because they shared so much blood, sweat and tears (literally).

The same is true for doctors. By now, you know to look at a doctor's curriculum vitae (CV), but we want to encourage you to take an even closer look than you might otherwise. There is a lot of useful information there. It is not as simple as just reading the CV through. Think about how to use that information. It can be a powerful connection for you to gain credibility and elevate your relationship. That means more sales.

Hint:

A customer is more likely to try your product if you can show that one of their mentors, friends, or colleagues is already using it. Are you doing your research?

Godfathers of Our Industries

Orthopedic Trauma:

> Dr. Ramon Gustillo
> Dr. Sigvard (Ted) Hanson Jr.

Orthopedic Recon:

> Sir John Charnley
> Dr. John Insall

Cardiac Surgery:

> Dr. Henry Souttar
> Dr. Michael DeBakey

Spine Surgery:

> Dr. Paul Harrington
> Dr. Arthur Steffe

Neurosurgery:

> Dr. Thor Sundt
> Dr. Gazi Yasargil

Consultative Selling

In consultative selling, you align with and relate to the needs of your customer and patient first, without worrying about making the sale. The value you add pays big dividends in time.

You already know you should be reading the same books and medical journals your customers do. So be sure you know which ones they are. If necessary, ask your doctors what they read and get your own subscription.

Once you are as well-informed as your customers, use that knowledge to leverage your situation. Do this by formulating good consultative selling questions.

They may sound something like this:

How many patients do you see with _____ [a given pathology] a week or a month? How are you currently treating those patients?

How do you currently treat patients with _____ [a given pathology]?

What case do you have on the books, that is keeping you up at night?

What do you consider your most complicated routine procedures?

Ultimately, you need to add value to your customer's practice. You want to be really helping, not just mining for information. For example, with the questions above, you should have something valuable to offer for the pathology you ask about. Knowing the true clinical and technical advantages of your products enables you to offer something real. You may even be able to make your customers aware of needs they don't realize they have.

There are many books about the art of consultative selling. Read as many as you can. Take the time to educate yourself, so when the opportunity comes to offer help, you can do it smoothly and gracefully.

Calling on Your Teammate

Resources

Once you decide you will start adding value to

your sales, where do you get the resources? And what is that value anyway?

Start by aligning yourself and your product with your surgeon's passions. It's not about financial gain. That takes care of itself. It's more about what will round out him or her professionally.

Marketing and Product Development

To stay abreast of the possibilities you can offer, keep your finger on the pulse of your own organization. Make sure to be first in line for data collection and product feedback. Provide valuable information to your sales and marketing departments as often as possible. The people in your organization urgently want surgeon and sales representative feedback. They begin by contacting those with whom they are comfortable. Part of your job is to make your marketing department comfortable with your doctors. It's a symbiotic relationship. They need your information and you need sales. Promote your customers. Become their agent, their "Jerry Maguire."

Professional Education

If your device industry is dependent on customer training, professional development is your gold mine. Constantly promote courses, speaking engagements, and training labs to your surgeons. This gives you more one-on-one time with them and truly is a huge value for them and their patients. When appropriate, don't forget to invite their staff, PAs, NPs, nurses, MAs, and so on. It's great for them as well. Professional education can be one of your most valuable consultative selling tools.

You can promote professional education without breaching the rules on event proctor selection. You simply have to constantly educate your internal colleagues about what your doctors are doing and what they are capable of doing.

Remember:

Busy surgeons make less money when they are away from their practice.

Company Bigwigs

When your company "bigwigs" come to town, don't be afraid to put them to work. It will impress your customers and it will impress the bigwigs too, as to how enterprising you are.

How do you arrange this? You're a top-notch salesperson. Sell them a great reason to come visit your customers. What's the benefit to them?

As the expression goes, "The squeaky wheel gets the grease." If you are persistent, executive visits to your customers are not only possible, they're probable. This meeting of the minds makes your customer feel truly important to you and to your company.

Create an action plan or follow-up plan before they leave town and don't be afraid to hold them accountable.

Tip:

When you pick up your bigwig from the airport, have in hand an agenda and CVs for all your doctors, along with your business plan.

Specialty Sales Teams

Why are companies investing in specialty sales teams and contracting teams? How can you harness their value and stay on their radar screen? These teams can make you money, so make the most of them.

These teams have goals. Find out what they are and do your utmost to help them achieve those goals. Once again, this requires aligning your surgeons internally. Lobby hard to get your facilities on the teams' target lists and covered in their overall strategies. Keep the teams engaged and up-to-date on what is happening in your facilities.

For more information about how to insert yourself into all aspects of the sale and to use the best parts of your corporation's sales model, we recommend the Bain & Company article, "Is Complexity Killing Your Sales Model?"[1]

Take Note: Specialty sales and contracting teams, according to Bain, are always current with the latest corporate developments. Stay close to them. They were designed and created to make you money. Plus, if you have any desire to move up in your organization, the contacts you make in these groups are invaluable. By monitoring the pulse of your company and the market as a whole, these internal relationships help you align your surgeon with important trends and priorities.

OTHER RESOURCES:

Textbooks

Sawbones

Anatomical Models

Product/Procedure Models

Education

Website Content

Search For Trained Providers

Patient Education Collateral

Educational Grants

Mission Trip Support

CHAPTER SUMMARY

• **The key to effective sales calls is preparation and planning.**

• Make time and manage it to grow your territory.

• Evaluate yourself objectively to see if you are doing everything you can to prepare for sales calls.

• Practice regular habits to stay fresh and prepared for sales opportunities.

• Know your customer. Study their CV. Make any connection you can via common acquaintances they went to school with. Build your "little black book" with detailed personal and professional information about each prospective customer.

• Get familiar with the many resources you have to grow your business and use them.

Chapter 4 Endnotes

[1] Dianne Ledingham, Mark Kovac, Michael Heric and Francois Montaville. "Is Complexity Killing Your Sales Model? How to build a repeatable, high-return sales model for business-to-business markets." Bain & Company.

Chapter 5

Playing Defense

Defending your Title

Ray's father used to say:

"If you win business with a bottle of scotch, you can lose business to a case of scotch." Moral of the story: You lose business the same way you win it. Remember this and you may stay out of trouble!

This is a very important chapter. We call it "Playing Defense" because you must defend your accounts. Just because you have a customer today doesn't mean you will tomorrow. It is never okay to become complacent with your account.

Your competition is not going away. They will keep attacking from every angle. The minute you begin to sit back and enjoy your commissions, your competitors will come in for the steal.

The best salespeople in the world have a healthy level of paranoia...at times even an unhealthy level.

Always Introduce New Technology Before Your Competition

Let's go a step further. The very worst way to lose a customer is to a competitor who sells a product, for which you have an almost identical solution.

That can easily happen when you get complacent. Say you have a customer who uses Product X. Then your company launches Product Y. You decide on your own that your customer is happy with Product X, so you never offer Product Y. Never mind that it looks cooler and works a little more easily.

Your thinking is, *If it ain't broke, why fix it?* Or maybe, *Why make more work for myself?*

A little later, your competitor shows up with a new technology very similar to your Product Y. It wows your customer and she gives all her business to your competitor...just because you never showed her that new product of yours.

John's Success Story:

We had a surgeon who was happy with our product. He was doing surgery in a relatively old-fashioned way. He was getting good outcomes and he was quick. He was happy with his sales rep and his service. In short, everything was going well.

Nevertheless, we showed him a new minimally invasive (MIS) solution, in a very non-threatening way. Here's how we presented it:

"We know you're satisfied with your current procedure, but we want to at least show you what is coming up on the horizon. Here is what people are doing with this product and what they are saying about it."

Over the next two years, we consistently kept showing him new iterations of this evolving product. It took time, but eventually this very conservative surgeon switched all of his surgeries over to the new minimally invasive technique. It has changed both his practice and his patients' outcomes.

This persistent process enabled us to upsell a more expensive product, while producing a less traumatic surgery.

You play good defense by systematically ensuring you always service your clients as if you don't have their business yet. You're always winning that business again.

Your customer may actually say, "Oh I'll NEVER use that." Don't accept their words at face value. You don't know what the future may hold.

Your competition may be introducing something similar and appearing to add value to their future sale. Make sure you show your customer first. Be the leader of the pack.

Even if your customer isn't buying right now, it's your responsibility to make sure he understands everything you have and everything you can do.

You can casually demonstrate a product without making it a sales call. Ask for his or her opinion on the product, as well as advice on how to position it with other doctors. Mention that you want his valuable feedback on the product, so that you can share it with your company.

Always remind your doctor, if he or she ever wants to learn a new technique or try something different, you are the person who does that.

Service, Service, Service

Remember that Michelin Guide star ranking comparison from Chapter 1? That's what this section is all about. Learn to be a three-star sales rep.

Add value to each and every individual who interacts with your products, invoices, or trainings. Start by defining each of the surgical team roles and understanding their training. Make sure your customer has the best product, instruments and training you can provide.

No matter how often your customer has turned them down in the past, keep offering Professional Education opportunities. Make sure your doctor and staff are connected to customer resources. This does not necessarily mean consulting agreements or teach/ faculty opportunities. It means:

• Any patient education literature your company can provide

• Educational links they can embed in their website

• Relationship building between your customer and other corporate departments, to help them feel a part of the greater good your organization does

Build a wall around your business and make it really difficult for your customers to leave, because they're getting so much added value.

Check your inventory to see what holes you have. Are you truly prepared to handle any emergency, revision, or removal? If not, this will be an avenue for your competition to make it into your OR. Think about it!

Develop a Healthy Paranoia

Keep your ears and eyes wide open at all times to see what's going on in the marketplace and what your competition is up to. There are always rumors and gossip going around. You don't have to get caught up in it, but do try to decipher what is credible and what is not.

You may hear about big purchasing agreements being negotiated or little trials your competitors are starting. You might learn about a new navigation system that works well with a competitor's product. You might even get wind of a new angio suite on the horizon.

Be wary that your competitor may partner with another company, to try to sneak into your hospital. Listen up!

Use ancillary staff as your eyes and ears. This is where all that relationship building you do pays big dividends. Your allies can become your undercover detectives.

Keep Your Friends Close and Your Enemies Even Closer

Keep your competition close. Know who they are and what their selling style is like. Know your competitors' product information as well as you know your own. Understand the corporate selling strategy your competition uses. Know where their sales force is focusing their efforts, as well as the incentives they are offering or receiving for certain products.

You never know when a little nugget of knowledge may turn the tide of a sale.

Another tip:

Your customer often lets down her guard when spending time with peers. Always attend dinners taking place at society meetings. You will hear their peers talk about what they are using and why. This is very, very valuable.

While you are attending that society meeting, make sure you walk the floor with your customer to look at all the other products. That's the time to see what catches their eye. And while you're at it, take them to your company booth for a warm welcome and lots of appreciative thank-you's for their business.

John's Story

When I had taken over a new region, the first person

I met at the door was Chris, the competitive sales rep. He took me out to have a coffee and made sure to find out all about me, my wife and kids. He was my best friend in the facility for two or three months. In fact, he even gave me suggestions for people to help me fill a role at our company.

Chris did a great job of knowing my every move, so he could be prepared to counter it. Unfortunately for him, we did still take a good chunk of business away from him, but he made it as difficult as possible. In a friendly way, of course.

You, the Expert

What does it mean to be an Expert on this playing field?

We define being an Expert as: being the very best sales representative in your territory, if not the state, region or country. An expert is the one the customer always calls on, because he's better and more knowledgeable than the local competition.

If you remember only one thing from this trusty little book, remember you must strive to be "The Expert" your doctors can rely on.

A key to playing defense is maintaining your Expert status. You may have won the business because you were at the right place at the right time, but that's not enough. Be the consultant. Add value and knowledge for your customer.

This doesn't stop after you make the sale. Ask yourself sincerely: Is your customer consulting you on clinical and technical decisions? What difficulties do they face that you can assist with?

Keep up with specialty journals, attend trade conferences and sit in on lectures (not at the booth). Learn new ways to sell your technologies at different angles. Stay up to date with the trends. You may decide to transfer your customers to different products.

Be careful, that you're not always biased toward your product. Defending your business doesn't mean just defending your product. Keep the patient's outcome in mind.

Sometimes a competitor may actually offer something which may make your customer's life easier. Are you mature enough to admit that to your customer? Will it build a stronger, more trusting relationship with that surgeon?

It's a scary thought, but it's something you have to think about.

Be Proactive, Rather than Reactive

Stay dynamic. Don't get lackadaisical. Push new technologies. Upsell.

While you are taking a break from showing your health care providers that new technology, your competition is probably taking that appointment time for themselves.

Remember your plan/strategy. On Monday

morning, do you get in your car and then start wondering where to go? Being proactive means planning ahead. Being reactive means racing to catch up.

Be proactive about staying current with industry and competitor information. Sign up for free Internet-based sources. Here are some great resources to use.

1. Mass Device - MassDevice.com

2. Google - Create Alerts on competitors

3. Orthopedics This Week - RYOrtho.com

4. Becker Orthopedic and Spine - BeckerOrthopedic.com

5. Cardiovascular Business - CardiovascularBusiness.com

Dig in and discover what new products are being developed. Sign up for FDA alerts indicating 510(k) clearances in your industry.

Ask your customers what they are reading. This is a great conversation opener at the scrub sink. When they tell you, be sure you read it too. Ask about their research, if they are at an academic center. This could be a great opportunity to drive a new product you were never thinking of for that customer.

We will say it again:

Stay Proactive

Always be looking ahead. Preventing problems is much easier than solving them.

Know when your contract is expiring. Know when your price increase may occur. Know when your customer is on vacation. Know when your customer is going to society meetings.

Don't let anything catch you by surprise, so you have to be reactive, rather than proactive.

Death of a Medtech Salesman?

You have probably read or heard over the past few years several articles about getting sales reps out of the OR. Most of this noise is surrounding price. In fact, there are even companies out there selling this model against you.

Below is an excerpt from the article, "Death of a Medtech Salesman," by Evan Anderson, 2012.

Adapt or Die

"Perhaps sales reps will ultimately be quoting Mark Twain: 'The reports of my death are greatly

81

exaggerated.' What is clear is that a significant shift is upon us, and reps' roles are changing. At Stanford Biodesign, one of the tenets of clinical need identification and screening is flushing out the stakeholders in order to target the decision-makers around a new technology and drive adoption. The power of stakeholders in healthcare is rapidly shifting and, to continue to be successful, we need to pivot and dig into their needs–not just in creating our sales strategy, but also in formulating the clinical need itself."

In short: The way to survive is to become a valuable source of knowledge that your customer can rely on.

CHAPTER SUMMARY

• Show your customer all your new technologies

• Provide unparalleled service and added value

• Keep your eyes and ears open, so you hear everything that may impact your account

• Maintain your expertise in the field through journals, meetings, and conferences

• Stay on top of internal and competitive technologies

In Conclusion...

In today's healthcare industry there is more opportunity than ever before. With the Affordable Care Act changing the business landscape at all levels of stakeholders, opportunity exists for innovation and creativity in medical device sales models.

We hope you enjoyed this short but powerful book. More important, we hope each and every one of you will put it to good use, make more money and gain more satisfaction from your careers as medical device sales consultants.

Now get out there and Improve Your Game!

Chapter 5 Endnotes

Mass Device – www.massdevice.com

Orthopedics This Week – www.ryortho.com

Becker's Orthopedic and Spine – www.beckerorthopedic.com

Cardiovascular Business – www.cardiovascularbusiness.com

"Death of a Medtech Salesman," by Evan Anderson, 2012

Bibliography

Preface:

Andy Molinsky, *Harvard Business Review* Feb 2016. "Practice for Tough Situations as You'd Practice a Sport"

Chapter 1:

Michelin Guide — www.viamichelin.com/web/restaurants

Anderson, ET. "Escaping the Discount Trap," *Harvard Business Review*, Sep 2013.

Daniel H. Pink, *Tß Sell Is Human: The Surprising Truth About Moving Others*

Carl Jung, *Psychological Types*, 1923

Barrick, M. R., Mount, M. K., & Judge, T. A. (2001) "Personality and performance at the beginning of the new millennium: What do we know and where do we go next?" *International Journal of Selection and Assessment*, 9, 9–30.

Adam M Grant, "Rethinking the Extraverted Sales Ideal: The Ambivert Advantage," Psychological Science, 24(6) 1024 –1030

Glengarry Glen Ross, 1992 New Line Cinema

Myers Briggs Type Indicator, www. myersbriggs. org

Chapter 2:

http://scholar.google.com/intl/en/scholar/about.html

AMA 2012 Physician Practice Benchmark Survey

Integrity Selling For The 21st Century, Ron Willingham

Atlas of Human Anatomy, Frank H. Netter

Small Business, "What Is a Sales Acumen?," by Carol Deeb

Handbook of Fractures, Egol and Koval

Spine Secrets, Vincent Devlin

Handbook of Neurosurgery, Greenberg Orthopedic Imaging, Greenspan Tarascon Pocket Orthopaedica, Rispoli Cardiology Essentials, Holler

Chapter 3:

AMA 2012 Physician Practice Benchmark Survey

Boston Healthcare, October, 2013, "Articulating the Value Proposition of Innovative Medical Technologies in the Healthcare Reform Landscape"

Chapter 4:

Dianne Ledingham, Mark Kovac, Michael Heric and Francois Montaville. "Is Complexity Killing Your Sales Model? How to build a repeatable, high-return sales model for business-to-business markets." Bain & Company

Chapter 5:

Mass Device – www.massdevice.com

Orthopedics This Week – www.ryortho.com

Becker's Orthopedic and Spine – www.beckerorthopedic.com

Cardiovascular Business – www.cardiovascularbusiness.com

"Death of a Medtech Salesman," by Evan Anderson, 2012

Printed in Great Britain
by Amazon